LISTENING FOR GOD
THROUGH
JAMES

Lectio Divina Bible Studies

wesleyan
publishing
house

Indianapolis, Indiana

Beacon Hill Press of Kansas City
Kansas City, Missouri

ABOUT THE
LECTIO DIVINA
BIBLE STUDIES

Lectio divina, Latin for *divine reading*, is the ancient Christian practice of communicating with God through the reading and study of Scripture. Throughout history, great Christian leaders including John Wesley have used and adapted this ancient method of interpreting Scripture. This Bible study builds on this practice, introducing modern readers of the Bible to the time-honored tradition of "listening for God" through His Word. In this series, the traditional *lectio divina* model has been revised and expanded for use in group Bible study. Each session in this study includes the following elements. (Latin equivalents are noted in italics.)

- Summary   A brief overview of the session.
  Epitome

- Silence   A time of quieting oneself prior to
  Silencio   reading the Word.

- Preparation   Focusing the mind on the central
  Praeparatio   theme of the text.

- Reading   Carefully reading a passage of
  Lectio   Scripture.

- Meditation   Exploring the meaning of the Bible
  Meditatio   passage.

- Contemplation   Yielding oneself to God's will.
  Contemplatio

- Prayer   Expressing praise, thanksgiving,
  Oratio   confession, or agreement to God.

- Incarnation   Resolving to act on the message of
  Incarnatio   Scripture.

The Lectio Divina Bible Studies invite readers to slow down, read Scripture, meditate upon it, and prayerfully respond to God's Word.

CONTENTS

INTRODUCTION

I magine if you had grown up in the shadow of your perfect half-brother Jesus. What would you have learned watching the God-man experience life a few years ahead of you? What would you have felt as He rose to prominence, commanded demons and illnesses to flee, and fed thousands with a little boy's lunch? What about as you watched public opinion turn against Him or as you watched Him die?

James, the author of this book, experienced these things. During Jesus' public ministry, younger brother James seems to have been a doubter (John 7:5). Yet the resurrected Christ appeared especially to this brother (1 Cor. 15:7), and James was among the believers as they gathered in the upper room in Acts 2. So, at some point, James became a true spiritual brother of his earthly brother.

After Peter's angelic deliverance from a Jerusalem jail, James assumed leadership of the Jerusalem church. His epistle may have been the first New Testament book written, as early as AD 45, a date before the Apostle Paul's ministry and before the influx of Gentiles into the church.

In style and tone, James often sounds much like Jesus. Compare, for example, James 1:12 with Jesus' words in Matthew 5:11–12. James uses Greek with ease, yet demonstrates an up-close knowledge of Jewish law. Some scholars speculate that the book may have originated as a collection of sermons.

Its content is focused on the practical, day-to-day living out of the example of Jesus, in word and in deed. One key theme is that the little sins we consider more acceptable (like gossip, jealousy, favoritism, and hoarding wealth) are as ugly in God's eyes as the biggies. This book also contains powerful challenges to stand firm in difficulty and to cultivate a fervent life of prayer. Its instructions have everything to do with how true believers—then and now—live as Christ-followers in the real world.

THE ROAD TO CHRISTIAN MATURITY

Listening for God through James 1:1–12

SUMMARY

The road to Christian maturity is not an easy path. It takes us through the difficult and unpleasant experiences of our human existence. Some of these experiences may be daily struggles of life commonly shared by all humanity. But other experiences go beyond the ordinary, and these we may find difficult, unbearable even. Regardless of the size of our struggles, we have the choice to allow them to hinder us or help us in our spiritual growth. The outcome depends on the way we encounter trials.

Trials of life, if encountered with uncertainty and wavering, will result in a defeated Christian life. This option will take us nowhere. Trials of life, if encountered with commitment and trust in God, will foster spiritual growth. This second road leads to a deep, satisfying life. James helps us discover this road to Christian maturity through today's reading.

SILENCE ✝ LISTEN FOR GOD

In silence, repeat the phrase, "I believe." Now listen to God's response as you commit to trust Him.

PREPARATION ✝ FOCUS YOUR THOUGHTS

How do you respond to the struggles of life? What is the level of your perseverance?

When you pray, do you pray with confidence that God will answer your prayer, or do you pray with uncertainty about God's answer?

READING ✝ HEAR THE WORD

James the Just, brother of Jesus, applies in this letter the foundational teachings of Jesus to specific situations that his audience faced in the middle of the first century. The suffering of the

Christian community is a key concern in this book of the Bible. James' goal is to challenge his audience to persevere in the midst of trials and to stand firm in their trust in God.

In this opening section, you will encounter the following words and phrases:

Servant: Though a leader, James sees himself as a slave called into the service of God.

The twelve tribes of Israel: James uses this term to describe believers.

Pure joy: A joy that is deep and overflowing.

Trials: The experience of suffering and hardship in life.

Perseverance: A firm, consistent display of faith and commitment.

Wisdom: A gift from God that gives a person the ability to discern God's plans.

Believe: The commitment to trust God.

Doubt: Wavering thoughts and actions despite a knowledge of the truth.

Crown of life: Eternal life.

Look for these phrases as you read James 1:1–12.

Read the sidebar quote from F. Mussner and reflect on the root cause of a person's inner conflict between the trust and distrust of God. Now reflect on a time or an event when you had the greatest

> The doubter is "one who lives in inner conflict between trust and distrust of God."
> —F. Mussner, quoted by Peter H. Davids

difficulty trusting God. How did you overcome that situation?

Meditate on James 1:9–11

James speaks about the poor and the rich. The present condition of the poor is deplorable, whereas the present condition of the rich is comfortable. Why do you think James speaks of the poor and the rich in this text? How do these verses relate to the preceding verses?

How can both poverty and wealth be a hindrance to trusting in God? What is James saying to Christians who are wealthy?

Read the sidebar quote from Jesus. Then read its context, Luke 18:18–25. Reflect on James' statement in light of the story of the rich ruler in Luke's Gospel.

> How hard it is for the rich to enter the kingdom of God!
> —Jesus (Luke 18:24)

Those who are preoccupied with their present circumstances may never truly know the joy that lies ahead. Yet the road to maturity invites us to have a broader perspective. What are the things you are preoccupied with these days? How do you see yourself? Are you poor or rich from God's perspective?

Meditate on James 1:12

God promises His children that perseverance through trials leads to the reward of eternal life. James' words here are a pronouncement of blessing and an invitation to those who become bogged down by the pressures of life and give up too quickly. What do you see as James' invitation to you in this verse? How would you explain the promise in this verse to someone who is struggling to maintain faith?

CONTEMPLATION ✝ REFLECT AND YIELD

How would your life be different if you were totally committed to trusting God in the midst of trials?

Do you see the present realities of your life with the broader perspective of God's will and purpose for your life? Are you open to the gift God has for you?

PRAYER † RESPOND TO GOD

James invites Christians to receive God's gift of wisdom—the Holy Spirit—to help us withstand the trials of life. Pray silently for God's gift. Pray with the certainty that God not only hears but will answer your prayer.

INCARNATION † LIVE THE WORD

God calls us not only to trust in Him but to lead others into a trusting relationship with Him. Think of someone you know who is easily bogged down by the struggles of life. Make a commitment to seek out that person and help him or her develop a stronger faith in God.

LIVING IN THE WORD

Listening for God through James 1:13–27

Epitome

SUMMARY

True Christian life is lived in the Word. Those who live in the Word know that God does not tempt His people. Rather He teaches them to avoid temptations. God's children, born through His truth, should live lives of self-control and practice discipline in speech and action.

For James, the key to this new birth and new way of life is being a hearer and doer of God's revealed Word. He calls us not only to hear the Word, but to follow it with action. Those who live in the Word practice true religion: a life of compassion for the poor in the world. This goes way beyond empty rituals.

In this section of James, you will discover the qualities of a life that is lived in the Word of God.

SILENCE ✝ LISTEN FOR GOD

In silence, meditate on the cross. Listen as God speaks to you through His Son.

PREPARATION ✝ FOCUS YOUR THOUGHTS

If you could choose a particular way of life, what would it be? Why would you make that choice? How different is that way of life from the way you live now?

READING ✝ HEAR THE WORD

After dealing with the issue of trials and the call to seek God's wisdom to withstand them, James reminds his readers that they should live by the Word through which God has given them life.

In this Scripture passage, you will encounter the following words and phrases:

Tempted: In Greek, this verb shares the same root word with the noun *trial*, but it conveys the added meaning of being enticed to sin.

Trial: In 1:2–12 a trial is an opportunity for spiritual maturity to develop.

Evil desire: Natural human desires that have been corrupted by sin.

Perfect law: The law of love that Jesus taught and practiced.

Religion: A human response to God through internal and external forms of worship.

World (Kosmos in the Greek): James here refers to the place of human existence that is corrupt and sinful.

Read James 1:13–27, paying special attention to these phrases in context.

MEDITATION ✝ ENGAGE THE WORD

Meditate on James 1:13–18

Trials offer the opportunity for growth. Yet trials, if misconstrued as temptations sent by God, will lead us to sin. Why do you think James insists on asserting that God does not tempt (test) anyone?

How do you respond to temptations? What are the areas of temptation to which you are most vulnerable? What do you do to overcome temptations?

Since temptations originate in one's evil desires, James calls people to take moral responsibility for their actions. Why do people often seek someone or something to blame for their actions? Have you ever succumbed to the temptation to blame someone else for your sin?

Compare James 1:4 with 1:15. Note that the God who gives us wisdom to withstand trials will not send temptations to mislead or cause us to fall into the trap of sin. How do these verses differ in the messages they communicate? What can you learn from reading them together?

What is the truth claim being made by the MasterCard ad in the sidebar? Compare it with the truth claim of James about the constancy of God. Why do you think James contrasts God's constancy with the lack of constancy in the sun and moon?

In a world of constant changes, one thing remains constant: MasterCard.
–TV Commercial

How does the Word (Jesus; see John 1:1) work in you to make you God's new creation?

Read the quote from Richard Foster and reflect on how Christ is formed in you. What does it mean to have Christ formed in you? What part do you have in the process?

> For the Christian heaven is not the goal, it is the destination. The goal is that Christ be formed in you.
>
> —Richard J. Foster

Meditate on James 1:19–21

The wisdom of God leads one to develop the disciplines of listening and speaking. Why is it important to listen carefully before we speak? Why is it important to speak cautiously and deliberately, with well-chosen words?

Think of a time when you have been quick to speak and slow to listen. What was the outcome? Now think of a time when you listened well and spoke few words. What was the outcome then?

James reminds his readers that humble submission to God's Word is the antidote to the poison of immorality. What does James mean by "humbly accept the word planted in you, which can save you"?

Meditate on James 1:22–25

Knowledge of the Word alone is not sufficient; hearing the Word without putting it into daily action is an act of self-deception. Why is it difficult to do what the Word says? What troubles have you experienced in this area?

For James, obedience is a way of life. What is this passage saying to people who have good intentions to obey God's Word, but often neglect to carry it out? What is this passage saying to people who have good intentions to obey God's Word, but act on their own terms?

How do the words of verse 25, "being not hearers who forget but doers who act" (NRSV), apply to you?

Meditate on James 1: 26–27

James connects true religion with ethical living, a life character-ized by disciplined speech, works of charity, service to the poor, and a total rejection of the evil influences of the world. How do these characteristics play out in your daily life? In what areas do you think God would have you improve? What word would you use to qualify or describe your practice of religion?

What does James mean when he concludes this section by reminding us to keep a "tight rein" on our tongues? What would others say about your speech?

Read and reflect on the words of Mother Teresa, a saintly woman of few words but great actions. How would your life change if you were to apply her words to your actions?

> We are supposed to preach without preaching not by words, but by our examples, by our actions.
> —Mother Teresa

CONTEMPLATION ✝ REFLECT AND YIELD

What are the benefits and blessings of a life lived in the Word? How would your life be changed if you became a person committed to ethical living through careful speech and compassionate deeds?

PRAYER ✟ RESPOND TO GOD

Living in the Word means being firmly planted in biblical truth. What is your present relationship to the Word through which God gave you a new birth? What are the influences of this world that keep you from faithfully living in the Word?

Pray silently and seek God's wisdom to say no to the temptations that come your way.

INCARNATION ✟ LIVE THE WORD

Think of a person whom you have offended by careless and angry words. Share with that person what God is saying to you and ask for forgiveness.

Think of a person who is among the neglected people in the world. Decide on at least one thing you will do to bring a blessing to that person.

KEEPING THE ROYAL LAW

Listening for God through James 2:1–13

SUMMARY

G od created all humanity in His image; all are equal in His sight. In our worldly perspective, we see the rich and the poor, the black and the white, the good looking and the not-so-good looking, the educated and the illiterate. The outcome of drawing such lines is the preferential treatment of one group at the expense of the other.

James saw favoritism as a critical problem in the Christian community of his day. In particular he was uncomfortable with preferential treatment of the rich at the expense of the poor. He says favoritism among God's people is a violation of God's command to love your neighbor as yourself. Breaking this commandment means breaking all of God's commandments.

What does it really mean to love your neighbor? Who is your neighbor?

SILENCE ✝ LISTEN FOR GOD

In silence, repeat the commandment: "Love your neighbor as yourself." Now listen as God speaks to you.

PREPARATION ✝ FOCUS YOUR THOUGHTS

What is your attitude toward wealth and poverty? What are your fears, if you are wealthy? What are your concerns if you are poor? What would you rather be: rich or poor? Why?

READING ✝ HEAR THE WORD

In this chapter James moves into another area of ethical living. He is concerned about those who call themselves Christians but practice discrimination against the poor. Ethical living calls for equal treatment of all regardless of economic or social status.

In this Scripture, you will encounter the following terms:

Poor: This term defined the identity of a Christian in the early church.

Your meeting: A gathering of the Christians. James uses the Greek term for synagogue, rather than *ekklesia,* the common term for church.

Kingdom: God's offer of salvation to the poor.

The rich: This term referred to those outside the Christian community.

The royal law: This term refers to Jesus' explicit commandment to "love your neighbor as yourself."

Mercy: A broad term that encompasses meeting the needs of others.

Consider how each of these terms applies to your own life as you read James 2:1–13.

MEDITATION ✝ ENGAGE THE WORD

Meditate on James 2:1–7

James calls on Christians to practice equal treatment of all who come to worship. Showing favoritism to those who are wealthy and treating the poor as second-class citizens indicate the practice of prejudice in the church. How is prejudice still an issue in the church today? How about in your own faith practice?

Why do you think James was concerned about the issue of favoritism? What is he saying to the church of his day that struggled with this issue?

How does James' statement about favoritism relate to a local church where the wealth/poverty difference is not as apparent? What are the indications of favoritism in the church today?

Read the sidebar quote by Mother Teresa. Why did she think the poor have so much to give to those who are not?

> We don't realize the greatness of the poor and how much they give us.
>
> —Mother Teresa

What does James mean when he says those who show favoritism have become "judges with evil thoughts"? How does favoritism become an evil act?

According to James, the poor who love God are heirs to His Kingdom, and thus they are rich from a spiritual perspective. What is James saying to Christians who may be poor in the eyes of the world today? What is James saying to Christians who may be wealthy in the eyes of the world today?

Compare James 2:5 with Matthew 5:3. See if Jesus' statement helps to offer further understanding of the requirements for one's inheritance of God's Kingdom. In what sense are you rich in your present relationship with God? How do you identify with the poor in the world?

Meditate on James 2:8–13

The royal law, "Love your neighbor as yourself" (Lev. 19:18), is a commandment found in a number of places in the New Testament. Why do you think this was an important guideline for early Christians?

Read Proverbs 14:21, and see how James tries to make a connection between the neighbor and the needy. What is the significance of this connection? What does it mean for you personally?

Read the sidebar quote by Aristides from the second century AD. How did Christians show their love for their neighbor? How did these actions make an impact on a watching world? What did they say about Christ through their actions toward orphans and the poor?

They love one another, and from widows they do not turn away their esteem; and they deliver the orphan from him who treats him harshly... And verily, this is a new people, and there is something divine in the midst of them.

—Aristides, a pagan, defending the Christians before Emperor Hadrian

Learning from James and early Christians, whom do you consider as your neighbor? What do you consider as the greatest commandment you follow?

James says breaking one law equals breaking all the laws of God. He also shows that our speech and conduct must be shaped by the conviction that the law that sets us free is also the law that convicts us. What is the law that gives us freedom? What place do you give to the royal law in your life?

What is James saying to those who think their acts of favoritism are not as serious as the sins of adultery or murder?

Read the quote from Richard Nixon. What does the image of black and white notes mean to you in the context of James' words on favoritism?

If you want to make beautiful music, you must play the black and the white notes together.

—Richard Nixon

What connection do you see between 2:3–4 and 2:13? What is the consequence of judgment without mercy? How do you see yourself in light of this Scripture? Can you think of an instance when mercy triumphed over judgment?

CONTEMPLATION ✝ REFLECT AND YIELD

What would your life be like if you were transformed by the call to show mercy and not favoritism? Are you ready to accept the challenge of James? Are you ready to make a decision to yield completely to the royal law?

PRAYER ✝ RESPOND TO GOD

The Gospels show that Jesus treated all people alike; in His eyes, there were no rich or poor. We live in a world that is sharply divided by race, socio-economics, and religious preferences. Pray silently, asking God to help you be like Jesus in this world.

INCARNATION ✝ LIVE THE WORD

What action will you take to practice the royal law today? What will you do to help others know the consequence of favoritism?

In what way will you become an agent of transformation in the church when you see judgment without mercy?

A LIVING FAITH

Listening for God through James 2:14–26

SUMMARY

Mother Teresa was invited to participate in a world conference on hunger in Bombay. She arrived at the conference building late because she got lost on the way. As she was going into the building, she saw a man lying in front of the door dying of hunger. She carried the man to the nearest home for the dying and missed the conference entirely. Imagine the irony of the situation. This man lay dying on the doorstep of the very building where representatives from powerful countries were confidently discussing plans to eliminate hunger in the next fifteen years.

Are we in the church more like the compassionate nun or the confident bureaucrats? We will find the answer in our actions, rather than our words. What do we do with our faith? Is it dead or alive? How do we know if our faith is dead or alive? If our faith is dead, how do we bring it to life? James invites us to ponder these questions, and transform our dead religion into a living, vibrant faith.

SILENCE ✝ LISTEN FOR GOD

In silence reflect on the incident from Mother Teresa's life. Listen as God speaks to you through this story.

PREPARATION ✝ FOCUS YOUR THOUGHTS

Why do you think others who went to the conference on hunger failed to notice the dying man on the doorstep? Why is it easy to have faith, but difficult to act? What would the world be like if the church actually lived out the example of Jesus Christ?

READING ✝ HEAR THE WORD

In this section James uses the literary device of a moral diatribe: a semi-conversational, question-and-implied-answer format that was popular in Greek communications. This device serves to establish his claim that if one has faith, it must be demonstrated through deeds of charity and righteousness.

In this Scripture, you will encounter the following terms:

Faith: The knowledge of the correct doctrine.

Deeds: This term also can be translated as *works*. (See Romans 11:6.) Paul uses this term to convey works of the law or legalistic observances, whereas in James, it means good deeds expected of a Christian.

Without clothes: This term refers to the outer garment needed to keep warm at night.

The scripture was fulfilled: This conveys the idea that one biblical text agrees with and supports another part of the Scriptures.

God's friend: The title *friend* for Abraham is found in 2 Chronicles 20:7 and Isaiah 41:8.

Rahab: An Old Testament example of hospitality to strangers. Her story appears in Joshua chapters 2 and 6.

Read James 2:14–26, listening for what God will say to you personally.

MEDITATION ✝ ENGAGE THE WORD

Meditate on James 2:14–17

James makes the solid claim that intellectual acceptance of orthodox doctrines unaccompanied by obedient actions cannot lead to
anything good. One can trust in Jesus as Savior, yet if this faith
is not put into action, it is not a living faith. Why does James say
faith without actions cannot save a person?

How would you describe James' understanding of salvation?
How do you relate what James is saying to the traditional notion
of salvation through one's trust in the faithfulness of God to save
us through Christ?

What understanding do you get about discipleship from this text?
How would you have responded if you were the person in James'
hypothetical example?

Read the sidebar quote by Francis
Beaumont. How does this analogy
apply to the Christian life?

> Faith without works
> is like a bird without
> wings; though she may
> hop with her companions on
> earth, yet she will never fly
> with them to heaven.
>
> —Francis Beaumont

What do you think James is saying here about the responsibility of the Christian community to those within the community who have physical needs? What would James say to a local Christian community where there may not be any serious physical need?

Some people think Christians should only be concerned with other Christians in need. How would you respond to this attitude?

Meditate on James 2:18–20

James anticipates an objection to his thesis that faith without works is dead. Some may think that faith and good deeds are unrelated to each other and that they are two different gifts. He argues that a good deed is the concrete proof of the existence of a faith that is alive. How do you respond to that statement?

What does James mean by "I will show you my faith by what I do"? What is the difference between sharing one's faith and showing one's faith? How would you best describe yourself, based on your answer to the previous question?

In verse 19, James introduces the most basic orthodox doctrine of Judaism: "There is one God." This is the Hebrew *Shema* (Deut. 6:4).

Why does James bring up this doctrine? Why do you think belief in one God is the starting point of Christian faith?

Read Deuteronomy 6:4–5. What is the primary duty of those who believe in one God? Why did Jesus connect the commandment to love God with the commandment to love one's neighbor? (See Mark 12:28–34.)

Meditate on James 2:21–26

In this section James introduces two illustrations to establish his claim that faith and deeds go together. What is James' objective when he cites the story of Abraham's offer of Isaac? What does James mean when he says, "His faith was made complete by what he did"?

Do you think there is a difference between righteousness that comes through actions and righteousness through faith?

Read Romans 4:3 and Galatians 3:6. What seems to be the point Paul is making in these passages? Both Paul and James quote the same Scripture (Gen. 15:6). Based on your encounter with what James has said so far, how does James interpret and use Genesis 15:6 as a support for his argument? What does James mean by his statement in verse 24? How does this text change your understanding of the relationship between faith, deeds, and salvation?

> In any well-proportioned life, there must be faith and works . . . If life is to be well-proportioned and fully effective in service and devotion, ·we must never think of it in terms of either or but always in terms of both and.
>
> —William Barclay

Read the sidebar quote by William Barclay. What does Barclay say about a balanced Christian life? How do you respond to his comment?

Based on verse 24, how would you describe your life and relationship with God?

Read Joshua 2:1–21 and Hebrews 11:31. Evaluate James' statement about the righteousness of Rahab in light of these two texts. How does her story add light to the subject of connecting faith and actions?

Read the Hannah More quote in the sidebar. How would you relate this message of the interconnectedness of faith and deeds to a person who thinks faith alone is necessary for salvation? To a person who has no faith but plenty of good deeds?

> If faith produces no works, I see that faith is not a living tree. Thus faith and works together grow, no separate life they never can know. They're soul and body, hand and heart. What God hath joined, let no man part.
>
> —Hannah More

CONTEMPLATION ✝ REFLECT AND YIELD

How would you characterize your faith? Is it a living faith or a dead faith?

If your life as a disciple of Jesus Christ is preoccupied with either faith or works only, accept the challenge to yield to the voice of God speaking through James.

PRAYER ✝ RESPOND TO GOD

In this passage James invites us to have a balanced understanding of the relationship between faith and good works. Faith without works is dead; works without faith are also dead. Pray silently for God to show you the practical importance of faith and works in your life as a disciple of Jesus Christ. Ask Him to give you opportunities to put feet to your faith.

INCARNATION ✝ LIVE THE WORD

Name someone you know in your community of faith who preaches faith without using words. Make an effort to pattern your life after that kind of practical expression of faith.

LIVING WITH AN ENEMY

Listening for God through James 3:1–12

SUMMARY

A ll of us know the destructive and poisonous power of an uncontrolled tongue. We daily witness strife and conflict in our human relationships caused by the words of a venom-laced tongue. In this lesson, James reminds us how this small organ in our body can cause big problems.

This small part of our body has the power to set our whole life on a path of destruction. If uncontrolled, the tongue can spread havoc like wild fire.

Yet the tongue, if controlled, can set life on its proper course. How is it possible to control the tongue? James says this humanly impossible thing is indeed possible. The power to control the tongue does not rest in human capacity; it comes as a gift from God. With God's help, you can indeed have victory over this enemy within you.

SILENCE ♰ LISTEN FOR GOD

In silence, repeat the words, "I am a child of God." Now listen for God's words which are grace-filled and grace-giving, words that come from the source of all wisdom.

PREPARATION ♰ FOCUS YOUR THOUGHTS

Do you speak often when you are in the company of others, feeling the need to be heard? Why?

What is your own assessment of your speech? If you could change one thing about your speech habit, what would it be?

Lectio
READING ✝ HEAR THE WORD

James leads us through a conversation about the power of the tongue. Though it is a small organ, the tongue has tremendous power. James is not appealing for silence but rather for speech that is controlled and beneficial to the whole community.

In this Scripture, you will encounter the following terms:

Teachers: Those entrusted with conveying the truth.

Stumble in many ways: Literally, we commit many sins.

Never at fault in what he says: One who has never sinned in his speech.

Keep . . . in check: To bridle.

Bits: Part of the bridle that keeps a horse under control.

Rudder: The person who controls it controls the ship.

A world of evil: The world of iniquity, as opposed to the world of truth and goodness.

God's likeness: Refers to humanity created in the image and likeness of God.

Read James 3:1–12, listening to what God will say to you in these powerful images.

MEDITATION ✝ ENGAGE THE WORD

Meditate on James 3:1–2

James begins this section with the warning that teaching in the Christian community is a responsibility that should be undertaken with utmost seriousness. Read Acts 15:24; 18:24–26; Romans 2:17–29; 1 Timothy 1:6–7; 6:3–5; 2 Timothy 4:3. What are the different types of teachers we find in these passages? What place did teachers have in early Christian faith? What was the greatest privilege of early Christian teachers?

What are some of the positive and negative influences teachers can have on their students? Why do you think James says teachers will be judged more strictly? What are the criteria by which teachers will be judged?

What is the greatest privilege of contemporary Christian teachers? Who were some of your teachers? What do you remember about them (your best and worst experiences)?

Read the sidebar quote from the Sayings of the Fathers. What might be the message of this ancient Jewish saying?

> He who multiplies words multiplies sin.
> —Sayings of the Fathers

In verse 2 James recognizes the universal problem of sin that affects all humanity. He also recognizes the reality that the most common sin is the sin caused by one's speech. He concludes that a person who has never been slipped up by his words is a perfect individual. However, the hypothetical nature of verse 2 shows the difficulty of attaining this virtue. Reread verse 2. What might James be saying about the relationship between perfection as a virtue and one's speech?

Meditate on James 3:3–6

Though the tongue is a small part of the human body, it has the greatest potential to be a positive influence upon the rest of the body. It can also lead to destructive and damaging consequences. How have you seen this play out in your own life?

James uses three illustrations in verses 3 –5 (bits, a rudder, and a spark) to make his point. How do these illustrations clarify James' message?

Think of a time when you failed to control your tongue when tensions were developing in your relationship with someone. What was its outcome?

Think of a time when you were cautious and controlled in your speech when tensions were developing in your relationship with someone. What was its outcome?

Why is it so difficult for most of us to control our tongue?

Read Proverbs 16:27, and relate its truth to verse 5.

James calls the tongue "the world of iniquity" among the other parts of the body. In what ways does the tongue corrupt the whole person?

An uncontrolled tongue not only corrupts the whole course of one's life, but it also wreaks havoc by setting one's life on fire. James says this fire comes from hell (*gehenna*), which is Satan's dominion. It is possible that James is tracing the destructive potential of the tongue to the power of Satan. How does this concept add to your understanding of the necessity to control the tongue?

Read the sidebar quote by Phillip Brooks. Though James is not advocating silence, when does silence prove more effective than speech?

> A man who lives right, and is right, has more power in his silence than another has by his words.
>
> —Phillip Brooks

Meditate on James 3:7–12

Human beings have demonstrated the capacity to tame and control all creatures God created. However, they have failed to show their ability to control the poisonous power of the tongue. How do the metaphors in verses 11 and 12 illustrate the overall message of James?

James concludes this section with an appeal to Christians that this cannot be the way of life for them—Christians cannot be double-tongued. Both praise and curse cannot come from the tongue of a Christian. How does that strong statement affect you?

Read the sidebar quote by Jesus. In what ways does Jesus' statement help us understand what James is saying?

> By their fruit you will recognize them. Do people pick grapes from thornbushes, or figs from thistles? Likewise every good tree bears good fruit, but a bad tree bears bad fruit. A good tree cannot bear bad fruit, and a bad tree cannot bear good fruit.
>
> —Jesus (Matt. 7:16–17)

James' discourse on the tongue is connected to his emphasis on perfect wisdom. (See James 1:5–8; 3:13–4:10.) Both of these passages deal with a double-minded person. (See 1:8 and 4:8.) What conclusion can you draw about the source of one's controlled tongue and pure speech?

If it is in our nature to have an unbridled tongue, how can we control our tongues—having only pure water proceeding from them? Where will we find the strength and ability to do this?

CONTEMPLATION ✝ REFLECT AND YIELD

What did God reveal to you concerning your tongue? How do you respond to James' admonition in verse 10: "Out of the same mouth come praise and cursing. My brothers [and sisters], this should not be." Are you willing to seek God's strength to control your tongue?

PRAYER ✝ RESPOND TO GOD

James instructs us on the damaging effect of an uncontrolled tongue. James also instructs on the need for pure speech that flows out of a pure heart.

Pray silently, and ask God to speak to you as you reflect on this Scripture.

INCARNATION ✝ LIVE THE WORD

Our speech should build up and not destroy others. Describe a specific course of action you will take to be more disciplined in your speech. Make a commitment to be a good listener, and speak only words that are full of grace.

A GRACE-FILLED LIFE

Listening for God through James 3:13–4:10

SUMMARY

There are two ways to live life. One alternative is to live in constant conflict with others. The other alternative is to live a life of peace and harmony with others. Conflict with others arises out of envy, selfish ambition, and a lack of humility. Lives lived in conflict are dictated by earthly wisdom, which promotes evil and disorder. Conversely, peace and harmony rule the lives of those who seek wisdom from above; such lives promote peace and righteousness in the world.

There is no middle ground, no third alterative or option, no place for a double-life. James invites us to live a life filled with grace and wisdom that the world cannot offer. By the help of God's grace, you can indeed live a life filled with peace, humility, and mercy—a life that is the antithesis of conflict and discord.

SILENCE ✝ LISTEN FOR GOD

In silence, meditate on the words, "Blessed are the peacemakers." Listen as God speaks to you.

PREPARATION ✝ FOCUS YOUR THOUGHTS

How do you see your own relationships with others? Are there conflicts and disharmony in your relationships? If so, what are you willing to do to bring peace and harmony with others?

READING ✝ HEAR THE WORD

James includes in his letter a collection of separate sayings, all focusing on the root causes of conflict in human relationships. He also instructs his readers regarding the actions they should take to bring peace and righteousness in the midst of chaos and disorder.

In this Scripture, you will encounter the following terms:

Wise and understanding: The combination of the words *wise* and *understanding* is found in a number of places in the Old

Testament. Using these terms James is addressing anyone who might pride himself as a teacher in the church.

Humility: A characteristic quality of teachers, stressed in the Jewish tradition.

Truth: In this context James may be referring to wisdom characterized by humility.

Unspiritual: In this context the word *unspiritual* refers to that which is physical.

Peace-loving, considerate, submissive, full of mercy and good fruit, impartial and sincere: These all are characteristic qualities of Christian life. (See Gal. 5:22.)

Harvest of righteousness: The fruit-bearing result of living a godly life.

Desires: By this word James means to draw our attention to the sinful and self-indulgent pleasures of our pre-Christ natures.

Grace: Though the word often means favor, here it may mean God's help.

Wash your hands . . . purify your hearts: A call not to external performance, but to inward transformation.

Thoughtfully and with spiritual ears listening for God's voice, read James 3:13–4:10.

MEDITATION ✝ ENGAGE THE WORD

Meditate on James 3:13–18

James reminds his readers that those who claim to have wisdom (those who claim to be teachers) need to show humility in their lives. How does James relate humility to wisdom? According to James, what is the true test of humility? What would be the outcome if good deeds are not done in a spirit of humility?

Read 1 Peter 2:12, and relate this verse to what James is saying in 3:13.

Read the quote from the Sayings of the Fathers addressed to teachers. This Jewish saying refers to the Torah as the source of wisdom. What is the relationship between James' words and this Jewish saying about the virtue of teachers?

> Lessen your labor for worldly goods, and occupy yourself with Torah; be humble of spirit before all men.
>
> —Sayings of the Fathers

True wisdom produces two things: good works and humility. James contrasts the wisdom of this world with the wisdom from above to illustrate the interconnectedness of wisdom, good works, and humility. List the character traits of those who have the wisdom that is of this earth (verses 14–16). What impact do these have on the community? List the character traits of those who have wisdom from above (verses 17–18). What impact do these have on the community?

Based on verse 18, what is the ultimate responsibility of those who claim to be wise and understanding (teachers) in the Christian community?

Meditate on James 4:1–6

In this section James turns his attention to the source of dissention and conflict within the Christian community. Desire, when it is not easily satisfied, leads to conflicts that affect relationships within the community. What connection does James see between unmet human desires and unanswered prayer?

Read Matthew 7:7–8, and relate these verses to James 4:3. How does James help us understand the teaching of Jesus? According to James, what kind of prayer does God not answer?

Read the sidebar quote by Garth Brooks. What is a prayer that you have prayed that was not answered? Are you now glad that your prayer was not answered?

> Sometimes the best prayers are the ones God does not answer.
>
> –Garth Brooks

Why do you think James addresses his audience as "adulterers"? How did James' audience prove to be friends of the world? How did friendship with the world impact their relationship with God? In what areas of your life do you find yourself in friendship with the world?

Verse 5 is difficult. Consult other translations for different readings of this verse. The NIV seems to give attention to the human spirit; a number of other translations read this verse as referring to God's jealousy for His people. How does each possible interpretation of this passage apply to your life?

James concludes this section with the reminder that God gives more grace, which is more than adequate to meet His divine requirement of humility. What difference does the grace of God make in your life? How does His grace equip and strengthen you to be a peacemaker?

Read the quote by John Selden. Why do you think people often talk about humility but seldom practice it?

> Humility is a virtue all preach, none practice; and yet everybody is content to hear.
>
> —John Selden

How does James contrast the proud and the humble in verse 6?

Meditate on James 4:7–10

There is only one way to deal with conflict and strife within the community of faith. What can one do to receive the gift of grace and the gift of wisdom?

James calls his audience double-minded. This seems to be James' favorite word for the spiritually unstable. Based on your reading of James 3:13–4:10, what causes double-mindedness among Christians?

Read 1 Peter 5:5–9. What similarities do you find between 1 Peter 5:5–9 and James 4:7–10? What do these two texts say about the practice of repentance in the early Christian community?

What specific actions do you take when you repent of sin? What is the response of God to those who humble themselves before Him?

CONTEMPLATION ✝ REFLECT AND YIELD

How would your relationship with others change if you received more grace from God?

How do you contribute to harmony and peace in your relationships? Are you ready to accept God's instructions to live a grace-filled life?

PRAYER ✝ RESPOND TO GOD

What are the things that cause you to be spiritually unstable? Pray silently and ask God to reveal the things that cause you to be double-minded.

INCARNATION ✝ LIVE THE WORD

God calls us not only to live in peace with others, but to be peacemakers. He also calls us to live grace-filled lives, in friendship with Him. List the things you will commit to do to fulfill God's purpose for your life.

JUDGMENT DAY IS COMING

Listening for God through James 4:11–5:6

SUMMARY

Love your neighbor as yourself. This is easier said than done. We may say we love our neighbor, but often our actions do not show it. We may say we love our neighbor, but often our neighbor is the subject of our slanderous conversations rather than the focus of our loving attention.

More often we love ourselves more than we love our neighbor. This is evident in the way we are preoccupied with material wealth and worldly pleasures.

James tells his readers why they should not judge others. He calls them to live a life depending on God's plans for them. And he teaches them what to do if they are pursuing a life preoccupied with wealth and riches. These words of wisdom call for actions that will put you on the right track with God.

SILENCE ✝ LISTEN FOR GOD

In silence, ask the question, "Am I living the Christian life?" Listen as God speaks to you about your present relationship with Him.

PREPARATION ✝ FOCUS YOUR THOUGHTS

Do you have a tendency to pass judgment on others?

Do you take control of your life and set the agenda for your future? Do you live a self-indulgent life with no thought of the coming judgment of God?

What would you want to change in these areas?

READING ✝ HEAR THE WORD

In this reading you will find James' instructions on keeping the law of love. Ultimately, this will be the basis of the final judgment.

In this Scripture you will encounter the following terms:

The law: most likely the royal law. (See James 2:8.)

The one who is able to save and destroy: This refers to God as the final judge and the one to whom people must make their appeal.

If the Lord wills: This statement indicates one's dependence on God and an acknowledgement that human life is in the hands of God.

Hoarded wealth: James may be using this phrase in an ironic way to mean storing up God's wrath.

Lord Almighty: the Old Testament form, *Lord Sabaoth* (The Lord of Hosts), depicts God as the commander of a great heavenly army.

Innocent men: the poor who are righteous.

Read James 4:11–5:6, paying special attention to these phrases.

MEDITATION ✝ ENGAGE THE WORD

Meditate on James 4:11–12

Slander has become a sickness that has affected our whole world. It spreads at epidemic pace particularly during election times. One cannot stand in line at the grocery store without observing headlines of tabloids that slander celebrities or politicians. James is concerned, in particular, with slander in the church. What are the different ways by which Christians in the first century might have slandered other Christians? (For example, consider the Jewish-Gentile make-up of the church. How would it have contributed to slander in the church?)

How do Christians slander other Christians today? Can you think of some examples?

James' concern for Christians is that they should keep the law of love. Those who pass judgment on others not only reject the call to love their neighbor, but they are also being critical of the law. Explain how this is so.

Read the sidebar quote from Jesus. How do you relate James' words to the words of Jesus? James warns those who slander and pass judgment on others that God alone is the only judge of all

> For in the same way you judge others, you will be judged, and with the measure you use, it will be measured to you.
> —Jesus (Matthew 7:2)

humanity. Why does James say only God is able to judge?

Read Isaiah 33:22, and relate the prophet's words to what James says about God.

Meditate on James 4:13–17

What is the attitude reflected in the words James quotes in verse 13?

James is not very concerned with the issues of making business plans or making money; trade and commerce were the primary livelihoods for many Christians in the first century. His concern is those who are arrogant and self-confident. Such arrogance almost always shows itself in one's capacity to control the events that lie ahead. How does this knowledge affect the plans you are making in your own life today?

Compare James 4:14b with Hosea 13:3. Hosea draws a similar analogy to describe the fate of the wicked. How do you respond to these analogies?

Though life is described elsewhere as transitory (see Ps. 90:5–6; Is. 40:6–8), James may be focusing here on the fate of the arrogant. What is the basic attitude of those who say the words quoted in verse 15? How do you know when these words simply become a meaningless religious formula and not real expression of humility before God?

With this in mind, can you think of instances when you have talked about God and His involvement in your future, but went ahead and made plans for yourself without seeking God's direction?

James reminds Christians that sin is not only bad things that we have done, but also our failure to do that which we have been commanded to do. Read the sidebar quote by Mother Teresa, which puts this statement into vivid context. What are the frequently committed sins

> At the end of life we will not be judged by how many diplomas we have received, how much money we have made, how many great things we have done. We will be judged by "I was hungry and you fed me, I was naked and you clothed me, I was homeless and you took me in."
>
> —Mother Teresa

of omission in the Christian life based on this quote? Which ones have you committed by omitting?

Meditate on James 5:1–6

James announces to his readers that the day of judgment has already come down upon the rich who hoard their wealth and oppress the poor. Compare James' reference to earthly treasure with Jesus' words in Matthew 6:19–20.

In the ancient culture hoarding wealth was a sin against the community because the wealthy were under obligation to give liberally to public and private needs. James uses words such as rotted, corroded, hoarded etc. What might James be saying about wealth that is not shared with others?

Read the quote by John Wesley. How does this help you formulate a proper perspective on money and stewardship?

Earn all you can, save all you can, give all you can.

—John Wesley

James reminds readers that God will bring His righteous judgment on those who have accumulated wealth by exploiting those who worked for them. Withholding fair wages from laborers is an act of injustice. Read Leviticus 19:13. See how this law is expanded in Deuteronomy 24:14–15. What do these Old Testament laws say about withholding wages from a laborer? How do they still apply to contemporary life?

In what ways do you see oppression of the poor by the rich in our world? How should the church respond when there is large-scale neglect and even exploitation of the poor in public and corporate economic policy?

CONTEMPLATION ✝ REFLECT AND YIELD

What changes need to take place in your life, in light of God's Word through James? Are you willing to accept the challenges found in this lesson?

PRAYER ✝ RESPOND TO GOD

The New Testament clearly teaches the truth that God's judgment is on all those who reject His call to love their neighbor. James instructs us not to pass judgment on others, not to be obsessed with our own life, and not to hoard wealth for our own pleasure-filled life. Pray silently, and wait for God to speak to you through this lesson.

INCARNATION ✝ LIVE THE WORD

The day of judgment should not be the reason for righteous living. If you are in a situation where others are violating the law of love by slandering another person, what can you do about it?

What would be a specific way you could share your wealth with others who need your help?

PATIENCE
AND PRAYER

Listening for God through James 5:7–20

SUMMARY

There is a huge scar on my stomach that reminds me every day that God intervened and saved me from a life-threatening infection when I was less than two months old. Doctors could provide no help. My parents told me the only thing they could do was pray and wait for God to heal me.

I believe in the power of prayer for healing. But I also believe we must wait patiently for God to carry out His will according to His good purposes.

James is a book on practical wisdom. In this last section of his book, James speaks on various issues that are important to your Christian life: Waiting for God. Maintaining integrity in speech.

Praying for the sick. Confessing sin. Doing everything to bring home those who have gone astray from their Christian faith.

SILENCE ✝ LISTEN FOR GOD

In silence, prepare your heart to hear God's Word through James. Meditate on the words of the Psalmist, "Wait for the Lord."

PREPARATION ✝ FOCUS YOUR THOUGHTS

What is your expectation when you pray for an urgent need? Are you willing to wait for God to respond in His time and according to His will?

READING ✝ HEAR THE WORD

James concludes his letter with some of his most practical instructions on Christlike living. He addresses issues of patience, swearing, prayer, healing, and seeking out the lost. In this Scripture you will encounter the following terms.

The Lord's coming: The Greek word *parousia* is the commonly used word in the New Testament for the Second Coming.

Elders: A well-established order of ministry in the early church; elders were spiritually mature men appointed to give spiritual guidance to the congregation.

Anoint him with oil: This means to symbolically set apart the sick person for God's special care and action.

Consider these phrases as you read James 5:7–20.

MEDITATION ✝ ENGAGE THE WORD

Meditate on James 5:7–11

What is your level of patience when you want to acquire something? How about your level of patience with others who may be somewhat slow in their actions?

Patience is a virtue, but not many people have it. Psalmists often call their readers to wait for the Lord (Ps. 27:14; 40:1). Waiting is a sign of one's patience. However, we also find the righteous crying out, "How long O Lord" (Ps. 13:1; Rev. 6:10)? Why do so many people lack patience? How does the consumerism in our world contribute to this lack of patience?

James admonishes his readers to wait patiently for the coming of the Lord—a much-anticipated event in the first century. Christians during this time believed they would be alive to see the coming of the Lord. How do you suppose this anticipation was heightened by the intensity of persecution they faced?

James calls Christians to imitate the farmer who waits patiently for the rains. Can you think of a time when you waited patiently for God to answer your prayer? Are there instances when you were impatient with God? How did your impatience impact your relationship with Him?

Read the sidebar quote by Barclay. What is the necessary ingredient for patience? How does knowing the character of God make it easier to wait for His answers to come?

> There will be moments in life when we think that God has forgotten, but if we cling to the remnants of faith, at the end of life we too shall see that God is very kind and very merciful.
>
> —William Barclay

Patience will reveal not only the purpose of God for His people during their trials but also prove that He is a compassionate and merciful God. How have you seen these character traits of God evidenced in your own life?

Meditate on James 5:12–18

Oath taking is a serious matter, as it guarantees the integrity of one's speech. However, frequent oath taking may become a way to avoid truth telling. Consider how often some people say, "I swear," after making a claim. How much credence do you put in the word of people who often feel the need to add this phrase to their statements?

Read the quote by Aeschylus. What is the emphasis of this quote?

> It is not the oath that makes us believe the man, but the man the oath.
>
> —Aeschylus
> (fifth-century Greek writer)

Integrity of speech seems to be the alternative to oath taking that James places before his readers. Where there is truthful speech, there is seldom any need for swearing. How does this knowledge affect the way you will speak in the future?

James concludes this section with instructions on prayer and healing. Why do you think James insists on involving the community of believers in prayer for healing? Why are some people in our day hesitant to ask for a public healing service? Why do they prefer anointing to be a private ritual?

In what ways have you been involved in praying for others, especially during their illnesses? What effect did prayer for their healing have in your life?

James seems to be associating illness with sin, a common religious concept in the Old Testament. Read the sidebar quote from Rabbi Alexandrai,

> No man gets up from his sickness until God has forgiven him all his sins.
>
> —Rabbi Alexandrai

which reflects the ancient Jewish understanding of the relationship between sin and sickness. Can you think of reasons some people in modern society may associate illness with sin?

What place does confession of sin have in your life? Why does James think confession of sin is necessary for healing? Why is it important to have a right relationship with God for people to recognize their physical, emotional, and spiritual health?

Meditate on James 5:19–20

James ends his letter with a charge to seek out those who have gone astray and left the Christian faith. Read Matthew 18:10–14. How does this text clarify James' admonition?

Read the quote from Proverbs 10:12. It is likely that James has this proverb in mind. What might be the final word he is giving to his readers? How do you relate this final verse to James' previous instruction to fulfill the royal law?

> Hatred stirs up dissension, but love covers over all wrongs.
> —Proverbs 10:12

CONTEMPLATION ✝ REFLECT AND YIELD

How will these instructions of James change the way you live and practice your faith? Are you willing to follow God's instructions for you?

PRAYER ✝ RESPOND TO GOD

Is faith that leads to patience at work in your life? What about truthfulness in speech?

Pray silently, and ask God to fill you with His patience and pure speech.

INCARNATION ✞ LIVE THE WORD

Think of a person who is ill in your faith community. Set aside time pray daily for the healing of that person. Take time to visit the person as well.

Commit to evidence your faith in daily life through consistent patience and truthful speech.

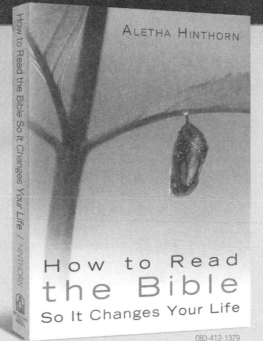

Get to know John Wesley and the spirit that ignited a passion for God!

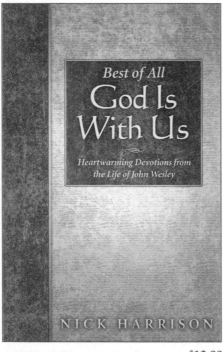

Mining gems from the heart of Wesley's writings, Nick Harrison presents 90 devotionals reflecting on subjects including prayer, stewardship, perfect love, and holiness.

These inspiring meditations present the founder of Methodism as a kindred spirit to Christians everywhere, reintroducing his amazing life and ministry while offering daily encouragement on the central issues of personal spirituality.

0-89827-317-X
Paperback

$12.99
192 pages